Taste of Home's
Gifts from a Jar

Publications International, Ltd.

ISBN: 1-4127-2366-3

Manufactured in China.

8 7 6 5 4 3 2 1

Microwave Cooking: Microwave ovens vary in wattage. Use the cooking times as guidelines and check for doneness before adding more time.

MEMORABLE GIFT GIVING

Create an unforgettable holiday gift for your friends and family by giving them a homemade gift jar filled with ingredients to make yummy cookies, bars, muffins, quick breads and cakes. Fill the jars as directed and add your personal decorating touch. The result—a beautiful gift that will make a lasting impression. Since most of the ingredients are premeasured and in the jar, recipe preparation is easier and more fun.

Keep the following tips in mind when preparing your gift jars.

• Always use a food-safe jar or container with an airtight lid.

• Use the jar size called for in the recipe. Check the jar size by filling the jar with water, 1 cup at a time. (4 cups = 1 quart; 6 cups = 1½ quarts)

• Make sure the jar or container is completely dry before filling it with ingredients.

• Measure all the ingredients accurately. Level off filled measuring cups with a metal spatula or knife.

• For ease in filling, use a wide-mouth jar if possible. Layer the ingredients into the jar using a use a canning funnel, if available, and a ¼-cup dry measuring cup, or the largest spoon that fits through the mouth of the jar. Tightly pack each layer to insure that all ingredients fit into the jar.

• Layer the ingredients in the jar according to the recipe directions. Fine ingredients such as flour and granulated sugar should be placed on the bottom when possible. They tend to cover up loosely layered ingredients such as chocolate chips or nuts. Brown sugar is a good separator for these ingredients.

• If not specified, pack brown sugar firmly in the jar. This will allow for all the ingredients to fit perfectly into the jar.

• Use small sandwich bags to hold ingredients as directed in some mix recipes. Close the bag with a twist tie, then cut off the top of the bag before placing it in the jar.

• Fill several jars at once for a make-ahead gift. Store filled jars in a cool place. You'll have a beautiful hostess or teacher gift ready to go.

• After the jar is filled, copy the preparation instructions on a decorative gift tag. Cover the top of the jar with a 9- or 10-inch circle of fabric. Tie the fabric and the gift tag onto the jar with raffia, ribbon, satin cord, string, yarn or lace.

• Put together more elaborate gifts by packing a gift basket with the ingredients needed to prepare the recipes. Add packages of beverages such as gourmet coffees and teas. Find beautiful cookie or cake plates, new baking pans and deluxe cooking utensils to create a memorable gift straight from the heart!

FAVORITE COOKIES

SUPER CHOCOLATE COOKIE MIX

1½ cups all-purpose flour
1 cup packed light brown sugar
¾ cup candy-coated chocolate pieces
½ cup salted peanuts
½ cup raisins
¼ cup unsweetened cocoa powder
¾ teaspoon baking soda
¼ teaspoon salt

1. Layer ingredients attractively in any order into 1-quart food storage jar with tight-fitting lid. Pack ingredients down lightly before adding another layer.

2. Cover top of jar with fabric; attach gift tag with raffia or ribbon.

Makes one 1-quart jar

SUPER CHOCOLATE COOKIES

⅔ cup butter, softened
2 eggs
1½ teaspoons vanilla
1 jar Super Chocolate Cookie Mix

1. Preheat oven to 350°F.

2. Beat butter in large bowl until smooth. Beat in eggs and vanilla until blended. (Mixture may appear curdled.) Add cookie mix to butter mixture; stir until well blended.

3. Drop heaping tablespoonfuls dough 2 inches apart onto ungreased cookie sheets. Bake 11 to 12 minutes or until almost set. Let cookies stand on cookie sheets 2 minutes. Remove cookies to wire racks to cool completely.

Makes 2 dozen cookies

GRANOLA COOKIE MIX

¾ cup all-purpose flour
½ teaspoon salt
½ teaspoon baking soda
½ teaspoon ground cinnamon
¾ cup packed brown sugar
 1 cup granola cereal
¾ cup semisweet chocolate chips
¾ cup raisins

1. Layer ingredients in 1-quart food storage jar with tight-fitting lid in following order: combined flour, salt, baking soda and cinnamon; brown sugar, lightly packed; granola; chocolate chips; and raisins.

2. Cover top of jar with fabric; attach gift tag with raffia or ribbon.

Makes one 1-quart jar

GRANOLA COOKIES

½ cup (1 stick) butter, softened
 1 egg
 1 jar Granola Cookie Mix
 1 tablespoon milk

1. Preheat oven to 350°F. Grease cookie sheets; set aside.

2. Beat butter in large bowl 1 minute with electric mixer at medium speed. Add egg; beat until well blended. Add contents of jar and milk; beat on low speed until well blended.

3. Drop dough by rounded tablespoonfuls 1½ inches apart onto prepared cookie sheets. Bake 10 to 12 minutes or until cookies are firm and lightly browned. Let stand on cookie sheets 2 minutes. Remove cookies to wire racks to cool completely.

Makes about 3 dozen cookies

Granola Cookies

CRISPY HOLIDAY TREAT MIX

1 cup powdered sugar
1½ cups crisp rice cereal
½ cup chopped dried tart cherries
¾ cup mini semisweet chocolate chips
¼ cup chopped toasted pecans
¾ cup flaked coconut

1. Layer all ingredients except coconut in the order listed above in 1-quart food storage jar with tight-fitting lid. Pack ingredients down firmly before adding another layer. Place coconut in small plastic food storage bag. Close with twist tie; cut off top of bag. Place bag in jar.

2. Cover top of jar with fabric; attach gift tag with raffia or ribbon.

Makes one 1-quart jar

CRISPY HOLIDAY TREATS

1 jar Crispy Holiday Treat Mix
1 cup peanut butter
¼ cup (½ stick) butter, softened

1. Remove coconut packet from jar. Place remaining contents of jar in large bowl; stir to blend. Combine peanut butter and butter in medium bowl, stirring until well blended. Add to cereal mixture; mix well.

2. Shape rounded teaspoonfuls of dough into 1½-inch balls. Roll balls in coconut. Place in single layer in large food storage container. Store in refrigerator.

Makes about 2 dozen treats

Serving Suggestion: Place balls in paper or foil candy cups. Candy cups are available in a variety of designs and colors at stores which carry cake decorating supplies.

Crispy Holiday Treats

Crispy Holiday Treats

1 jar Crispy Holiday Treats Mix
1 cup peanut butter
¼ cup butter, softened

1. Remove coconut packet from jar. Place remaining contents of jar in la... blend. Combine peanut butter in medi... wl, stirring until ... Add to cereal mixture. Stir until well blended ...

2. Shape generous teaspoonfuls of dough ... 2-inch balls. Roll ball... in single layer in large food storage con... Store in refrigerat... ...dies in par... ...lors at s...

Serving Suggestion: Place indiv... available in a variety of design...

CHERRY PISTACHIO BISCOTTI MIX

1½ cups all-purpose flour
1¼ teaspoons baking powder
½ teaspoon salt
½ teaspoon ground ginger
½ teaspoon ground cinnamon
½ cup dried tart cherries or chopped apricots
½ cup packed brown sugar
¼ cup granulated sugar
½ cup pistachio nuts or almonds, toasted*
2 tablespoons coarse decorating or granulated sugar

*To toast nuts, spread in single layer on baking sheet. Bake in preheated 350°F oven 8 to 10 minutes or until golden brown, stirring frequently.

1. Layer all ingredients except coarse sugar in the order listed above in 1-quart food storage jar with tight-fitting lid. Lightly pack down ingredients before adding another layer. Place coarse sugar in small plastic food storage bag. Close with twist tie; cut off top of bag. Place bag in jar.

2. Cover top of jar with fabric; attach gift tag with raffia or ribbon.

Makes one 1-quart jar

Cook's Note: Coarse decorating sugar can be found in most supermarkets and many specialty food stores.

Gift Idea: Assemble a gift basket with a jar of Cherry Pistachio Biscotti Mix and a holiday tin to store the baked biscotti. Add a package of premium coffee or tea.

CHERRY PISTACHIO BISCOTTI

1 jar Cherry Pistachio Biscotti Mix
¼ cup (½ stick) butter, cut into pieces
1 egg
2 tablespoons milk or almond-flavored liqueur
1 teaspoon almond extract or vanilla

1. Preheat oven to 350°F. Lightly grease cookie sheet.

2. Remove sugar packet from jar. Place remaining contents of jar in large bowl; stir until well blended. Cut in butter with pastry blender or two knives until mixture resembles coarse crumbs. Whisk together egg, milk and almond extract in small bowl. Add to flour mixture, stirring to form stiff dough. Knead dough in bowl. Divide dough in half; shape into two 9×2-inch logs. Place 2 inches apart on prepared cookie sheet. Sprinkle sugar evenly over each log.

3. Bake 25 minutes or until logs are lightly browned. Cool logs on wire rack 15 minutes. *Reduce heat to 325°F.* Slice each log diagonally into ¾-inch-thick slices. Place slices, cut side up, on cookie sheet. Bake 10 minutes; turn biscotti over. Bake 5 to 10 minutes or until surfaces are golden brown and cookies are dry. Remove biscotti to wire racks; cool completely. *Makes about 1½ dozen biscotti*

Cherry Pistachio Biscotti

HAPPY BIRTHDAY COOKIE MIX

1¼ cups flour
½ teaspoon baking powder
¼ teaspoon baking soda
¼ teaspoon salt
⅓ cup packed brown sugar
⅓ cup granulated sugar
½ cup chocolate-covered toffee chips
¾ cup mini candy-coated chocolate pieces
½ cup peanut butter and milk chocolate chips
½ cup lightly salted peanuts, coarsely chopped

1. Combine flour, baking powder, baking soda and salt in large bowl. Spoon flour mixture into 1-quart food storage jar with tight-fitting lid. Layer remaining ingredients on top of flour. Pack ingredients down lightly before adding another layer.

2. Cover top of jar with fabric; attach gift tag with raffia or ribbon.

Makes one 1-quart jar

HAPPY BIRTHDAY COOKIES

½ cup (1 stick) butter, softened
1 egg
½ teaspoon vanilla
1 jar Happy Birthday Cookie Mix

1. Preheat oven to 375°F. Line cookie sheets with parchment paper.

2. Beat butter in large bowl until fluffy. Beat in egg and vanilla. Add contents of jar to butter mixture; beat 1 minute or until light dough forms.

3. Drop dough by rounded tablespoonfuls 2 inches apart onto prepared cookie sheets. Bake 10 minutes or until firm and golden brown. Let stand on cookie sheets 1 minute. Remove cookies to wire racks to cool completely.

Makes 3 dozen cookies

Happy Birthday Cookies

Happy Birthday Cookies

½ cup (1 stick) butter, softened
1 egg

½ teaspoon vanilla
1 jar Happy Birthday Cookie Mix

1. Preheat oven to 375°F. Line cookie sheets with parchment paper.

2. Cream butter until light. Beat in egg and vanilla. Pour contents of jar into butter mixture. Beat 1 minute or until light dough forms.

3. Drop dough by rounded tablespoons 2 inches apart onto cookie sheet. Bake 10 minutes or until firm and golden brown. Let cookies stand 1 minute. Remove to wire racks; cool completely.

Makes 3 dozen cookies

DOUBLE CHOCOLATE PEANUT BUTTER COOKIE MIX

1¾ cups all-purpose flour
1 cup packed brown sugar
¾ cup mini candy-coated chocolate pieces
¾ cup peanut butter and milk chocolate chips
¼ cup unsweetened cocoa powder
¾ teaspoon baking soda
½ teaspoon salt

1. Layer ingredients attractively in any order into 1-quart food storage jar with tight-fitting lid. Pack ingredients down tightly before adding another layer.

2. Cover top of jar with fabric; attach gift tag with raffia or ribbon.

Makes one 1-quart jar

DOUBLE CHOCOLATE PEANUT BUTTER COOKIES

¾ cup (1½ sticks) butter, softened
½ cup peanut butter
2 eggs
½ teaspoon vanilla
1 jar Double Chocolate Peanut Butter Cookie Mix

1. Preheat oven to 350°F.

2. Beat butter and peanut butter in large bowl until smooth. Beat in eggs and vanilla until blended. Add cookie mix; stir until well blended.

3. Drop dough by rounded tablespoonfuls 2 inches apart onto ungreased cookie sheets. Bake 8 to 10 minutes or until almost set. Let cookies stand on cookie sheets 1 minute. Remove cookies to wire racks to cool completely.

Makes about 4 dozen cookies

Double Chocolate Peanut Butter Cookies

Double Chocolate Peanut Butter Cookies

¾ cup (1½ sticks) butter, softened
⅓ cup peanut butter
2 eggs
½ teaspoon vanilla
1 jar Double Chocolate
Butter Cook!

FRUIT AND NUT CHIPPERS MIX

1¼ cups all-purpose flour
¾ cup packed brown sugar
1 cup milk chocolate chips
½ cup chopped dried apricots
½ cup chopped pecans or walnuts
½ teaspoon baking soda
¼ teaspoon salt

1. Layer ingredients attractively in any order into 1-quart food storage jar with tight-fitting lid. Lightly pack down ingredients before adding another layer.

2. Cover top of jar with fabric; attach gift tag with raffia or ribbon.

Makes one 1-quart jar

FRUIT AND NUT CHIPPERS

½ cup (1 stick) butter, softened
1 egg
½ teaspoon vanilla
1 jar Fruit and Nut Chippers Mix

1. Preheat oven to 350°F.

2. Beat butter in large bowl until smooth. Beat in egg and vanilla until blended. (Mixture may appear curdled.) Add contents of jar to butter mixture; stir until well blended.

3. Drop dough by heaping teaspoonfuls 2 inches apart onto ungreased cookie sheets. Bake 9 to 10 minutes or until edges are golden brown. Let cookies stand on cookie sheets 2 minutes. Remove cookies to wire racks to cool completely.

Makes about 3 dozen cookies

Fruit and Nut Chippers

COWBOY COOKIE MIX

1 cup all-purpose flour
1 cup uncooked old-fashioned oats
¾ cup semisweet chocolate chips
½ cup packed light brown sugar
½ cup chopped nuts
½ cup seedless and/or golden raisins
¼ cup granulated sugar
2 tablespoons unsweetened cocoa powder
½ teaspoon baking powder
¼ teaspoon baking soda

1. Layer ingredients attractively in any order into 1-quart food storage jar with tight-fitting lid. Pack ingredients down lightly before adding another layer.

2. Cover top of jar with fabric; attach gift tag with raffia or ribbon.

Makes one 1-quart jar

COWBOY COOKIES

½ cup (1 stick) butter, softened
1 egg
1 teaspoon vanilla
1 jar Cowboy Cookie Mix

1. Preheat oven to 350°F. Lightly grease cookie sheets.

2. Beat butter in large bowl until smooth. Beat in egg and vanilla until blended. (Mixture may appear curdled.) Add cookie mix to butter mixture; stir until well blended.

3. Drop dough by rounded tablespoonfuls 2 inches apart onto prepared cookie sheets. Bake 12 to 14 minutes or until edges are lightly browned. Remove to wire racks to cool completely.

Makes about 2½ dozen cookies

Cowboy Cookies

TRACY'S PIZZA PAN COOKIE MIX

1½ cups all-purpose flour
1¼ cups semisweet chocolate chips
¾ cup packed brown sugar
½ cup chopped walnuts or pecans
½ teaspoon baking soda
¼ teaspoon salt

1. Layer ingredients attractively in any order into 1-quart food storage jar with tight-fitting lid. Lightly pack down ingredients before adding another layer.

2. Cover top of jar with fabric; attach gift tag with raffia or ribbon.

Makes one 1-quart jar

TRACY'S PIZZA PAN COOKIE

½ cup (1 stick) butter, softened
4 ounces cream cheese, softened
1 egg
½ teaspoon vanilla
1 jar Tracy's Pizza Pan Cookie Mix

1. Preheat oven to 350°F. Lightly grease 12-inch pizza pan.

2. Beat butter and cream cheese in large bowl until smooth. Beat in egg and vanilla until blended. (Mixture may appear curdled.) Add cookie mix to butter mixture; stir until well blended. Press dough evenly into prepared pan.

3. Bake 12 to 15 minutes or until lightly browned on top. Cool completely in pan on wire rack. To serve, cut into wedges.

Makes one 12-inch cookie

Tracy's Pizza Pan Cookie

ULTIMATE CHIPPERS MIX

1¼ cups all-purpose flour
½ cup packed light brown sugar
½ cup semisweet chocolate chips
½ cup milk chocolate chips
½ cup white chocolate chips
¼ cup granulated sugar
¼ cup coarsely chopped pecans
½ teaspoon baking soda
¼ teaspoon salt

1. Layer ingredients attractively in any order into 1-quart food storage jar with tight-fitting lid. Pack ingredients down lightly before adding another layer.

2. Cover top of jar with fabric; attach gift tag with raffia or ribbon.

Makes one 1-quart jar

ULTIMATE CHIPPERS

½ cup (1 stick) butter, softened
1 egg
1½ teaspoons vanilla
1 jar Ultimate Chippers Mix

1. Preheat oven to 375°F.

2. Beat butter in large bowl until smooth. Beat in egg and vanilla until blended. (Mixture may appear curdled.) Add cookie mix to butter mixture; stir until well blended.

3. Drop heaping teaspoonfuls of dough 2 inches apart onto ungreased cookie sheets. Bake 10 to 12 minutes or until edges are golden brown. Let cookies stand on cookie sheets 2 minutes. Remove cookies to wire racks to cool completely.

Makes 4 dozen cookies

Ultimate Chippers

LUSCIOUS BARS

MYSTICAL BAR MIX

1 cup graham cracker crumbs
1 cup coarsely chopped pecans
¾ cup flaked coconut
¾ cup semisweet chocolate chips
½ cup uncooked old-fashioned or quick oats
½ cup raisins

1. Layer ingredients attractively in any order into 1-quart food storage jar with tight-fitting lid. Pack ingredients down tightly before adding another layer.

2. Cover top of jar with fabric; attach gift tag with raffia or ribbon.

Makes one 1-quart jar

MYSTICAL BARS

⅓ cup butter
1 jar Mystical Bar Mix
1 can (14 ounces) sweetened condensed milk

1. Preheat oven to 350°F. Melt butter in 13×9-inch baking pan. Remove from oven.

2. Place contents of jar in large bowl. Add sweetened condensed milk; stir with spoon until well blended.

3. Spread batter evenly over butter in prepared pan. Bake 22 to 25 minutes or until lightly browned. Cool completely in pan on wire rack 5 minutes. Cut into bars.

Makes 2½ dozen bars

APRICOT ALMOND BAR MIX

1¾ cups all-purpose flour
2 teaspoons baking powder
1 cup chopped dried apricots or dried cherries
½ cup packed brown sugar
1 cup powdered sugar, divided
⅓ cup sliced almonds

1. Layer flour, baking powder, apricots, brown sugar and ½ cup powdered sugar in 1-quart food storage jar with tight-fitting lid. Lightly pack down ingredients before adding another layer. Place remaining ½ cup powdered sugar and almonds in separate small plastic food storage bags. Close each bag with twist tie; cut off tops of bags. Place in jar.

2. Cover top of jar with fabric; attach gift tag with raffia or ribbon.

Makes one 1-quart jar

APRICOT ALMOND BARS

1 jar Apricot Almond Bar Mix
½ cup (1 stick) butter, softened
1 egg
1 teaspoon almond extract
1½ teaspoons milk

1. Preheat oven to 350°F. Grease 13×9-inch baking pan.

2. Remove powdered sugar and almond packets from jar. Place remaining contents of jar in medium bowl; stir until well blended. Beat butter, egg and extract in large bowl with electric mixer on medium speed. (Mixture may appear curdled.) Add flour mixture; beat until just blended. (Dough will be crumbly.) Press dough into prepared pan; sprinkle with almonds. Bake 25 minutes until lightly browned. Cool in pan on wire rack.

3. Place powdered sugar in small bowl. Add enough milk to make glaze, stirring until smooth. Drizzle over warm cookies. Cool completely in pan on wire rack.

Makes about 3 to 4 dozen bars

Serving Suggestion: To cut these delicious bars into diamond shapes, cut straight lines 1 inch apart the length of the pan. Then, cut straight lines 1½ inches apart diagonally across the pan.

Apricot Almond Bars

CHOCOLATE RASPBERRY BAR MIX

1⅓ cups all-purpose flour
1 cup packed brown sugar
1 cup uncooked quick or old-fashioned oats
⅔ cup mini chocolate-coated candy pieces
⅓ cup unsweetened cocoa powder
1 teaspoon baking powder
½ teaspoon salt
¼ teaspoon baking soda

1. Layer ingredients attractively in any order into 1-quart food storage jar with tight-fitting lid. Pack ingredients down tightly before adding another layer.

2. Cover top of jar with fabric; attach gift tag with raffia or ribbon.

Makes one 1-quart jar

CHOCOLATE RASPBERRY BARS

½ cup (1 stick) butter, softened
2 eggs
1 jar Chocolate Raspberry Bar Mix
⅓ cup seedless raspberry jam

1. Preheat oven to 350°F. Grease 9-inch square baking pan.

2. Beat butter in large bowl until smooth. Beat in eggs until blended. (Mixture may appear curdled.) Add contents of jar to butter mixture; stir until well blended.

3. Reserve 1 cup dough; spread remaining dough into prepared pan. Spread preserves evenly over dough to within ½ inch of edges of pan. Drop teaspoonfuls of reserved dough over preserves.

4. Bake 25 to 30 minutes or until bars are slightly firm near edges. Cool completely in pan on wire rack.

Makes 16 bars

Chocolate Raspberry Bars

ROCKY ROAD BROWNIE MIX

1 cup sugar
1 cup coarsely chopped walnuts
1 cup semisweet chocolate chips
½ cup all-purpose flour
½ cup unsweetened cocoa powder
1 cup miniature marshmallows

1. Layer all ingredients except marshmallows attractively in any order into 1-quart food storage jar with tight-fitting lid. Pack ingredients down lightly before adding another layer. Place marshmallows in resealable plastic food storage bag; seal. Place bag in jar.

2. Cover top of jar with fabric; attach gift tag with raffia or ribbon.

Makes one 1-quart jar

ROCKY ROAD BROWNIES

1 jar Rocky Road Brownie Mix
½ cup (1 stick) butter, melted
¼ cup buttermilk
1 egg
1 teaspoon vanilla

1. Preheat oven to 350°F. Lightly grease 8-inch square baking pan. Remove marshmallows from jar; set aside.

2. Place remaining brownie mix in large bowl. Add melted butter, buttermilk, egg and vanilla; stir until well blended.

3. Spread batter evenly in prepared pan. Bake 25 to 30 minutes or until set. Sprinkle with reserved marshmallows. Bake 3 to 5 minutes or until marshmallows are puffed and slightly melted. Cool in pan on wire rack.

Makes 16 brownies

Rocky Road Brownies

PEANUT BUTTER CHIP BROWNIE MIX

> 1 cup all-purpose flour
> 1 cup packed brown sugar
> ¾ cup peanut butter chips
> ½ cup granulated sugar
> ½ cup chopped peanuts
> ⅓ cup unsweetened cocoa powder
> ½ teaspoon baking powder
> ¼ teaspoon salt

1. Layer ingredients attractively in any order in 1-quart food storage jar with tight-fitting lid. Pack ingredients down slightly before adding another layer.

2. Cover top of jar with fabric; attach gift tag with raffia or ribbon.

Makes one 1-quart jar

PEANUT BUTTER CHIP BROWNIES

> 1 jar Peanut Butter Chip Brownie Mix
> ½ cup (1 stick) butter, melted
> 2 eggs, lightly beaten

1. Preheat oven to 350°F. Grease 8-inch square baking pan.

2. Pour contents of jar into large bowl. Combine butter and eggs in small bowl until blended; stir into jar mixture until well blended. Spread evenly in prepared pan.

3. Bake 30 to 35 minutes or until edges begin to pull away from sides of pan. Cool in pan on wire rack.

Makes 16 brownies

Peanut Butter Chip Brownies

CARAMEL CHOCOLATE CHUNK BLONDIE MIX

1½ cups all-purpose flour
1 cup semisweet chocolate chunks
¾ cup granulated sugar
¾ cup packed brown sugar
1 teaspoon baking powder
½ teaspoon salt

1. Layer ingredients attractively in any order into 1-quart food storage jar with tight-fitting lid. Pack ingredients down tightly before adding another layer.

2. Cover top of jar with fabric; attach gift tag with raffia or ribbon.

Makes one 1-quart jar

CARAMEL CHOCOLATE CHUNK BLONDIES

½ cup (1 stick) butter, softened
2 eggs
1½ teaspoons vanilla
1 jar Caramel Chocolate Chunk Blondie Mix
⅓ cup caramel ice cream topping

1. Preheat oven to 350°F. Grease 13×9-inch baking pan.

2. Beat butter in large bowl until smooth. Beat in eggs and vanilla until blended. (Mixture may appear curdled.) Add contents of jar to butter mixture; stir until well blended.

3. Spread batter evenly in prepared pan. Drop spoonfuls of caramel topping over batter; swirl into batter with knife. Bake 25 minutes or until golden brown. Cool in pan on wire rack.

Makes 2½ dozen blondies

Caramel Chocolate Chunk Blondies

SNOWY DATE NUT SQUARES MIX

1¼ cups all-purpose flour
1 teaspoon dried orange peel
½ teaspoon baking powder
¼ teaspoon baking soda
¼ teaspoon salt
¼ teaspoon ground cinnamon
¼ teaspoon ground nutmeg
⅛ teaspoon ground cloves
1½ cups (8 ounces) finely chopped dates
¼ cup packed brown sugar
¼ cup granulated sugar
½ cup finely chopped toasted walnuts*
1 cup powdered sugar

Place nuts in a microwavable dish. Microwave on HIGH 1 to 2 minutes or just until light golden brown, stirring nuts every 30 seconds. Allow to stand 3 minutes. Cool completely before chopping.

1. Layer all ingredients except powdered sugar in the order listed above in wide mouth 1-quart food storage jar with tight-fitting lid. Lightly pack down ingredients before adding another layer. Place powdered sugar in small plastic food storage bag. Close with twist tie; cut off top of bag. Place bag in jar.

2. Cover top of jar with fabric; attach gift tag with raffia or ribbon.

Makes one 1-quart jar

SNOWY DATE NUT SQUARES

1 jar Snowy Date Nut Squares Mix
½ cup (1 stick) butter, softened
2 eggs
2 tablespoons orange juice

1. Preheat oven to 350°F. Spray 8-inch square baking pan with nonstick cooking spray.

2. Remove powdered sugar packet from jar; set aside. Pour remaining contents of jar into large bowl; stir until well blended. Beat butter in medium bowl with electric mixer on medium speed until smooth. Beat in eggs, one at a time. (Mixture may appear curdled.) Beat in orange juice. Add butter mixture to date-nut mixture; stir until well blended. Spread batter into prepared pan.

3. Bake 25 to 30 minutes or until toothpick inserted into center comes out clean. Cool slightly in pan on wire rack; cut into 1-inch squares. Place powdered sugar in small bowl. Roll warm cookies in powdered sugar; coat well.

Makes 3 dozen squares

Snowy Date Nut Squares

COCOA BROWNIE MIX

1¼ cups all-purpose flour
1 cup granulated sugar
¾ cup packed light brown sugar
⅔ cup unsweetened cocoa powder
½ cup chopped walnuts
1 teaspoon baking powder
¼ teaspoon salt

1. Layer ingredients attractively in any order in 1-quart food storage jar with tight-fitting lid. (Pack ingredients down lightly before adding another layer.)

2. Cover top of jar with fabric; attach gift tag with raffia or ribbon.

Makes one 1-quart jar

COCOA BROWNIES

¾ cup (1½ sticks) butter, softened
3 eggs
1½ teaspoons vanilla
1 jar Cocoa Brownie Mix

1. Preheat oven to 350°F. Lightly grease 13×9-inch baking pan.

2. Beat butter in large bowl until smooth. Beat in eggs and vanilla until blended. (Mixture may appear curdled.) Add contents of jar to butter mixture; stir until well blended.

3. Spread batter evenly in prepared pan. Bake 20 to 25 minutes or until brownies spring back when lightly touched. Do not overbake. Cool in pan on wire rack.

Makes about 2½ dozen brownies

Cocoa Brownies

NO-FUSS BAR COOKIE MIX

2 cups graham cracker crumbs
1 cup flaked coconut
1 cup semisweet chocolate chips
½ cup coarsely chopped walnuts

1. Layer ingredients attractively in any order into 1-quart food storage jar with tight-fitting lid. Pack ingredients down lightly before adding another layer.

2. Cover top of jar with fabric; attach gift tag with raffia or ribbon.

Makes one 1-quart jar

NO-FUSS BAR COOKIES

1 jar No-Fuss Bar Cookie Mix
1 can (14 ounces) sweetened condensed milk

1. Preheat oven to 350°F. Lightly grease 13×9-inch baking pan.

2. Place bar contents of jar in large bowl. Add sweetened condensed milk; stir with spoon until well blended.

3. Spread batter evenly in prepared pan. Bake 15 to 18 minutes or until edges are golden brown. Cool completely in pan on wire rack.

Makes 2 dozen bars

No-Fuss Bar Cookies

TANGY LEMONADE BAR MIX

2¼ cups all-purpose flour
1 cup sugar
1 cup dried cranberries
1 tablespoon grated lemon peel
¾ teaspoon baking soda
¾ teaspoon salt

1. Layer ingredients attractively in any order into 1½-quart food storage jar with tight-fitting lid. Pack ingredients down lightly before adding another layer.

2. Cover top of jar with fabric; attach gift tag with raffia or ribbon.

Makes one 1½-quart jar

TANGY LEMONADE BARS

½ cup (1 stick) butter, softened
⅓ cup thawed frozen lemonade concentrate
1 egg
1 jar Tangy Lemonade Bar Mix

1. Preheat oven to 375°F. Lightly grease 13×9-inch baking pan.

2. Beat butter in large bowl until smooth. Beat in lemonade concentrate and egg until blended. (Mixture may appear curdled.) Add contents of jar to butter mixture; stir until well blended.

3. Press dough evenly in prepared pan. Bake 20 to 25 minutes or until golden. Cool completely in pan on wire rack.

Makes 2½ dozen bars

Tangy Lemonade Bars

MARVELOUS MUFFINS

CRANBERRY-PECAN MUFFIN MIX

1¾ cups all-purpose flour
1 cup dried cranberries
¾ cup chopped pecans
½ cup packed light brown sugar
2½ teaspoons baking powder
½ teaspoon salt

1. Layer ingredients attractively in any order in 1-quart food storage jar with tight-fitting lid. Pack ingredients down lightly before adding another layer.

2. Cover top of jar with fabric; attach gift tag with raffia or ribbon.

Makes one 1-quart jar

CRANBERRY-PECAN MUFFINS

1 jar Cranberry-Pecan Muffin Mix
¾ cup milk
¼ cup (½ stick) butter, melted
1 egg, beaten

1. Preheat oven to 400°F. Grease or paper-line 12 standard (2½-inch) muffin pan cups.

2. Pour contents of jar into large bowl. Combine milk, melted butter and egg in small bowl until blended; stir into jar mixture just until moistened. Spoon evenly into prepared muffin cups.

3. Bake 16 to 18 minutes or until toothpick inserted into centers comes out clean. Cool in pan on wire rack 5 minutes. Remove from pan; cool completely on wire rack.

Makes 1 dozen muffins

Cranberry Pecan Muffins

¼ cup butter, melted
1 egg, beaten

Cranberry Pecan Muffin Mix
⅓ cup milk

1. Preheat oven to 400°F. Grease or paper-line 12 regular-size (2½-inch) muffin cups.
2. Empty contents of jar into large bowl. Combine butter, milk and egg in small bowl until blended. Stir into jar mixture just until moistened. Spoon evenly into prepared muffin cups.
3. Bake 14 to 16 minutes or until toothpick inserted in centers comes out clean. Cool cakes in pan on rack 5 minutes; remove from pan and cool completely on wire rack.
Makes 12 muffins

APPLE RAISIN MUFFIN MIX

1½ cups all-purpose flour
1 cup chopped dried apples
⅔ cup packed brown sugar
½ cup uncooked old-fashioned oats
½ cup chopped walnuts
½ cup raisins
1 tablespoon baking powder
1 teaspoon ground cinnamon
½ teaspoon salt
⅛ teaspoon ground nutmeg
⅛ teaspoon ground ginger

1. Layer ingredients attractively in any order in 1-quart food storage jar with tight-fitting lid. Pack ingredients down lightly before adding another layer.

2. Cover top of jar with fabric; attach gift tag with raffia or ribbon.

Makes one 1-quart jar

APPLE RAISIN MUFFINS

1 jar Apple Raisin Muffin Mix
½ cup milk
½ cup (1 stick) butter, melted
2 eggs

1. Preheat oven to 400°F. Grease or paper-line 12 standard (2½-inch) muffin pan cups.

2. Pour contents of jar into large bowl. Combine milk, butter and eggs in small bowl until blended; stir into jar mixture just until moistened. Spoon evenly into prepared muffin cups, filling about ⅔ full.

3. Bake 15 to 17 minutes or until toothpick inserted into centers comes out clean. Remove from pan; cool completely on wire rack.

Makes 1 dozen muffins

Apple Raisin Muffins

PUMPKIN CHOCOLATE CHIP MUFFIN MIX

2½ cups all-purpose flour
1 cup packed light brown sugar
1 cup semisweet chocolate chips
½ cup chopped walnuts
1 tablespoon baking powder
1½ teaspoons pumpkin pie spice*
¼ teaspoon salt

Substitute ¾ teaspoon ground cinnamon, ⅛ teaspoon ground ginger and scant ¼ teaspoon each ground allspice and ground nutmeg for 1½ teaspoons pumpkin pie spice.

1. Layer ingredients attractively in any order in 1-quart food storage jar with tight-fitting lid. Pack ingredients down lightly before adding another layer.

2. Cover top of jar with fabric; attach gift tag with raffia or ribbon.

Makes one 1-quart jar

PUMPKIN CHOCOLATE CHIP MUFFINS

1 jar Pumpkin Chocolate Chip Muffin Mix
1 cup solid-pack pumpkin (not pumpkin pie filling)
¾ cup milk
6 tablespoons butter, melted
2 eggs

1. Preheat oven to 400°F. Grease or paper-line 18 standard (2½-inch) muffin pan cups.

2. Pour contents of jar into large bowl. Combine pumpkin, milk, butter and eggs in small bowl until blended; stir into jar mixture just until moistened. Spoon evenly into prepared muffin cups, filling ⅔ full.

3. Bake 15 to 17 minutes or until toothpick inserted into centers comes out clean. Cool in pans on wire racks 10 minutes. Remove from pans; cool completely on wire racks.

Makes 1½ dozen muffins

Pumpkin Chocolate Chip Muffins

BANANA CHOCOLATE MINI MUFFIN MIX

2¼ cups all-purpose flour
1 cup packed brown sugar
1 cup mini chocolate-coated candy pieces or mini chocolate chips
2 teaspoons baking powder
½ teaspoon salt

1. Layer ingredients attractively in any order into 1-quart food storage jar with tight-fitting lid. Pack ingredients down tightly before adding another layer.

2. Cover top of jar with fabric; attach gift tag with raffia or ribbon.

Makes one 1-quart jar

BANANA CHOCOLATE MINI MUFFINS

1 jar Banana Chip Mini Muffin Mix
1 cup mashed ripe bananas (about 2 large)
½ cup (1 stick) butter, melted
2 eggs
½ teaspoon vanilla

1. Preheat oven to 350°F. Grease or paper-line 36 mini (1¾-inch) muffin pan cups.

2. Pour contents of jar into large bowl. Combine bananas, butter, eggs and vanilla in medium bowl until blended; stir into jar mixture just until moistened. Spoon evenly into prepared muffin cups, filling almost full.

3. Bake about 15 minutes or until tops are golden brown and toothpick inserted into centers comes out clean. Cool in pans on wire racks 5 minutes. Remove from pans; cool completely on wire racks.

Makes 3 dozen mini muffins

Banana Chocolate Mini Muffins

TOFFEE DELIGHT MUFFIN MIX

3 cups all-purpose flour
⅔ cup packed brown sugar
1 package (8 ounces) toffee baking bits
1 tablespoon baking powder
1 teaspoon baking soda
½ teaspoon salt

1. Layer ingredients attractively in any order in 1-quart food storage jar with tight-fitting lid. Pack ingredients down firmly before adding another layer.

2. Cover top of jar with fabric; attach gift tag with raffia or ribbon.

Makes one 1-quart jar

TOFFEE DELIGHT MUFFINS

1 jar Toffee Delight Muffin Mix
1 cup milk
1 cup sour cream
6 tablespoons butter, melted
2 eggs
2 teaspoons vanilla

1. Preheat oven to 400°F. Grease or paper-line 24 standard (2½-inch) muffin pan cups.

2. Pour contents of jar into large bowl. Combine milk, sour cream, butter, eggs and vanilla in small bowl until blended; stir into jar mixture just until moistened. Spoon evenly into prepared muffin cups, filling ⅔ full.

3. Bake 16 to 18 minutes or until toothpick inserted into centers comes out clean. Remove from pans; cool 10 minutes on wire racks. Serve warm or cool completely.

Makes 2 dozen muffins

Toffee Delight Muffins

GRANOLA SPICE MUFFIN MIX

2¾ cups all-purpose flour
¾ cup sugar
⅔ cup granola cereal
½ cup raisins
1 tablespoon baking powder
1 teaspoon ground cinnamon
½ teaspoon salt
¼ teaspoon ground nutmeg
⅛ teaspoon ground allspice

1. Layer ingredients attractively in any order in 1-quart food storage jar with tight-fitting lid. Pack ingredients down tightly before adding another layer.

2. Cover top of jar with fabric; attach gift tag with raffia or ribbon.

Makes one 1-quart jar

GRANOLA SPICE MUFFINS

1 jar Granola Spice Muffin Mix
1½ cups milk
6 tablespoons vegetable oil
2 eggs
Coarse decorating sugar (optional)

1. Preheat oven to 400°F. Grease or paper-line 18 standard (2½-inch) muffin pan cups.

2. Place contents of jar in large bowl. Combine milk, oil and eggs in small bowl until blended; stir into jar mixture just until moistened. Spoon evenly into prepared muffin cups. Sprinkle with coarse sugar, if desired.

3. Bake 15 to 17 minutes or until toothpick inserted into centers comes out clean. Remove from pans; cool completely on wire racks. *Makes 1½ dozen muffins*

Granola Spice Muffins

PUMPKIN SPICE MINI MUFFIN MIX

2 cups all-purpose flour
2 teaspoons baking powder
¾ teaspoon salt
½ teaspoon baking soda
½ teaspoon ground ginger
¼ teaspoon ground nutmeg
¼ teaspoon ground cloves
¾ cup chopped dried cranberries
½ cup brown sugar
¼ cup granulated sugar
1 teaspoon ground cinnamon

1. Layer all ingredients except granulated sugar and cinnamon in the order listed above in 1-quart food storage jar with tight-fitting lid. Pack ingredients down before adding another layer. Combine granulated sugar and cinnamon in small plastic food storage bag. Close with twist tie; cut off top of bag. Place bag in jar.

2. Cover top of jar with fabric; attach gift tag with raffia or ribbon.

Makes one 1-quart jar

Gift Idea: Assemble a holiday celebration basket with a jar of Pumpkin Spice Muffin Mix, a package of gourmet coffee or tea and 3 mini (12-cup) muffin pans.

PUMPKIN SPICE MINI MUFFINS

1 jar Pumpkin Spice Mini Muffin Mix
½ cup (1 stick) butter, softened
1 cup solid-pack pumpkin
2 eggs
½ cup orange juice
1 teaspoon vanilla

1. Preheat oven to 400°F. Grease or paper-line 36 mini (1¾-inch) or 12 standard (2½-inch) muffin pan cups.

2. Remove sugar packet from jar; set aside. Place remaining contents of jar in large bowl; stir until well blended. Beat butter in medium bowl with electric mixer at medium speed until creamy. Beat in pumpkin, eggs, orange juice and vanilla until well blended. (Mixture may appear curdled.) Add to flour mixture; stir just until moistened. Spoon evenly into prepared muffin cups, filling cup ¾ full.

3. Bake 12 to 15 minutes or until toothpick inserted into centers comes out clean. Remove muffins from pans. Place sugar mixture in small bowl. Roll warm muffins in sugar mixture to coat. Serve immediately.　　*Makes 3 dozen mini muffins*

Pumpkin Spice Mini Muffins

FRUITY GINGERBREAD MUFFIN MIX

        1¾ cups all-purpose flour
         1 cup chopped dried mixed fruit bits
         1 cup chopped nuts
        ⅓ cup sugar
         2 teaspoons baking powder
        ¾ teaspoon ground ginger
        ¼ teaspoon salt
        ¼ teaspoon baking soda
        ¼ teaspoon ground cinnamon

1. Layer ingredients attractively in any order in 1-quart food storage jar with tight-fitting lid. Pack ingredients down lightly before adding another layer.

2. Cover top of jar with fabric; attach gift tag with raffia or ribbon.

Makes one 1-quart jar

FRUITY GINGERBREAD MUFFINS

         1 jar Fruity Gingerbread Muffin Mix
        ½ cup milk
        ⅓ cup vegetable oil
        ¼ cup light molasses
         1 egg

1. Preheat oven to 375°F. Grease or paper-line 12 standard (2½-inch) muffin pan cups.

2. Pour contents of jar into large bowl. Combine milk, oil, molasses and egg in medium bowl. Stir milk mixture into flour mixture just until moistened. Spoon evenly into prepared muffin cups, filling ⅔ full.

3. Bake 15 to 18 minutes or until toothpick inserted into centers comes out clean. Remove from pan; cool on wire rack 10 minutes. Serve warm or cold.

Makes 1 dozen muffins

Fruity Gingerbread Muffins

SWEET POTATO MUFFIN MIX

2 cups all-purpose flour
1 tablespoon baking powder
1 teaspoon ground cinnamon
½ teaspoon baking soda
½ teaspoon salt
¼ teaspoon ground nutmeg
½ cup packed brown sugar
¾ cup chopped walnuts
¾ cup golden raisins

1. Combine flour, baking powder, cinnamon, baking soda, salt and nutmeg in large bowl. Layer flour mixture, brown sugar, walnuts and raisins in 1-quart food storage jar with tight-fitting lid. Pack ingredients down slightly before adding each layer.

2. Cover top of jar with fabric; attach gift tag to jar with raffia or ribbon.

Makes one 1-quart jar

SWEET POTATO MUFFINS

1 cup cooked, mashed sweet potato
¾ cup milk
½ cup (1 stick) butter, melted
2 eggs, beaten
1½ teaspoons vanilla
1 jar Sweet Potato Muffin Mix

1. Preheat oven to 400°F. Grease or paper-line 24 standard (2½-inch) muffin pan cups.

2. Combine sweet potato, milk, butter, eggs and vanilla in large bowl. Stir in contents of jar just until combined. Spoon batter evenly into prepared muffin cups.

3. Bake 15 minutes or until toothpick inserted into centers comes out clean. Cool in pans 5 minutes; remove to wire racks.

Makes 2 dozen muffins

Sweet Potato Muffins

CINNAMON-RAISIN MUFFIN MIX

⅓ cup granulated sugar
⅓ cup packed brown sugar
1¼ cups all-purpose flour
1½ teaspoons baking powder
1 teaspoon ground cinnamon
½ teaspoon ground allspice
½ teaspoon ground nutmeg
¼ teaspoon salt
1 cup uncooked quick oats
1 cup raisins

1. Layer ingredients in 1-quart food storage jar with tight-fitting lid in following order: granulated sugar; brown sugar, lightly packed; combined flour, baking powder, cinnamon, allspice, nutmeg and salt; oats; and raisins.

2. Cover top of jar with fabric. Attach gift tag to jar with raffia and ribbon.

Makes one 1-quart jar

CINNAMON-RAISIN MUFFINS

⅔ cup milk
⅓ cup butter, melted
1 egg
1 jar Cinnamon-Raisin Muffin Mix

1. Preheat oven to 400°F. Grease or paper-line 12 standard (2½-inch) muffin pan cups.

2. Combine milk, butter and egg in medium bowl; whisk until well blended. Place contents of jar in large bowl; mix well. Add milk mixture; stir until just blended. Fill prepared muffin cups ⅔ full with batter.

3. Bake 14 to 15 minutes or until toothpick inserted into centers comes out clean. Cool 15 minutes in pan on wire rack.

Makes 1 dozen muffins

Cinnamon-Raisin Muffins

BOUNTIFUL BREADS

CRANBERRY CORN BREAD MIX

1½ cups all-purpose flour
1 cup yellow cornmeal
1 cup dried cranberries
½ cup sugar
2 teaspoons baking powder
½ teaspoon baking soda
½ teaspoon salt

1. Layer ingredients attractively in any order in 1-quart food storage jar with tight-fitting lid. Pack ingredients down lightly before adding another layer.

2. Cover top of jar with fabric; attach gift tag with raffia or ribbon.

Makes one 1-quart jar

CRANBERRY CORN BREAD

1 jar Cranberry Corn Bread Mix
½ cup shortening
1⅓ cups buttermilk
2 eggs

1. Preheat oven to 350°F. Spray 8½×4½-inch loaf pan with nonstick cooking spray.

2. Pour contents of jar into large bowl. Cut in shortening with pastry blender or two knives until mixture resembles coarse crumbs. Beat buttermilk and eggs in small bowl until blended. Add to shortening mixture; stir until mixture forms stiff batter. (Batter will be lumpy.) Pour into prepared pan, spreading evenly and removing any air bubbles.

3. Bake 45 to 50 minutes or until toothpick inserted in center comes out clean. Cool in pan on wire rack 10 minutes. Remove from pan; cool 10 minutes on wire rack. Serve warm.

Makes 1 loaf

APRICOT-CRANBERRY BREAD MIX

2½ cups all-purpose flour
1 cup chopped dried apricots
¾ cup sugar
½ cup dried cranberries
4 teaspoons baking powder
½ teaspoon baking soda
½ teaspoon salt

1. Layer ingredients attractively in any order in 1-quart food storage jar with tight-fitting lid. Pack ingredients down lightly before adding another layer.

2. Cover top of jar with fabric; attach gift tag with raffia or ribbon.

Makes one 1-quart jar

APRICOT-CRANBERRY BREAD

1 jar Apricot-Cranberry Bread Mix
1¼ cups buttermilk
¼ cup shortening
1 egg, beaten

1. Preheat oven to 350°F. Spray 9×5-inch loaf pan with nonstick cooking spray.

2. Pour contents of jar into large bowl. Combine buttermilk, shortening and egg in small bowl until blended; stir into jar mixture just until moistened. Pour evenly into prepared pan.

3. Bake 45 to 50 minutes or until toothpick inserted into center comes out clean. Cool in pan on wire rack 10 minutes. Remove bread from pan; cool completely on wire rack.

Makes 1 loaf

Apricot-Cranberry Bread

PEANUT BUTTER CHOCOLATE CHIP BREAD MIX

3 cups all-purpose flour
1 cup mini semisweet chocolate chips
½ cup granulated sugar
½ cup packed light brown sugar
1½ teaspoons baking powder
1 teaspoon baking soda
½ teaspoon salt

1. Layer ingredients attractively in any order in 1-quart food storage jar with tight-fitting lid. Pack ingredients down lightly before adding another layer.

2. Cover top of jar with fabric; attach gift tag with raffia or ribbon.

Makes one 1-quart jar

PEANUT BUTTER CHOCOLATE CHIP BREAD

1 jar Peanut Butter Chocolate Chip Bread Mix
1 cup creamy peanut butter
½ cup (1 stick) butter, softened
2 eggs
2 teaspoons vanilla
1½ cups buttermilk

1. Preheat oven to 350°F. Spray two 8½×4½-inch loaf pans with nonstick cooking spray.

2. Combine peanut butter and butter in large bowl; beat with electric mixer at medium speed until light and fluffy. Add eggs, one at a time, beating well after each addition. Beat in vanilla. Add contents of jar alternately with buttermilk, beating at low speed after each addition until blended. Divide batter evenly between prepared loaf pans.

3. Bake about 45 minutes or until toothpick inserted into centers come out clean. Cool in pans on wire racks 10 minutes. Remove from pans; cool completely on wire racks.

Makes 2 loaves

Peanut Butter Chocolate Chip Bread

BLACK FOREST BANANA BREAD MIX

1¾ cups all-purpose flour
1 cup semisweet chocolate chips
¾ cup chopped pecans
⅔ cup packed brown sugar
2 teaspoons baking powder
½ teaspoon salt

1. Layer ingredients attractively in any order into 1-quart food storage jar with tight-fitting lid. Pack ingredients down tightly before adding another layer.

2. Cover top of jar with fabric; attach gift tag with raffia or ribbon.

Makes one 1-quart jar

BLACK FOREST BANANA BREAD

1 jar (10 ounces) maraschino cherries
⅓ cup butter, softened
1 cup mashed ripe bananas (about 2 large)
2 eggs
1 jar Black Forest Banana Bread Mix

1. Preheat oven to 350°F. Lightly spray 9×5-inch loaf pan with nonstick cooking spray.

2. Drain cherries, reserving 2 tablespoons juice. Coarsely chop cherries.

3. Beat butter in large bowl until smooth. Beat in bananas, eggs and reserved cherry juice until well blended. Add bread mix and chopped cherries to butter mixture; stir until blended. Pour evenly into prepared pan.

4. Bake 1 hour or until golden brown and toothpick inserted into center comes out clean. Cool in pan on wire rack 10 minutes. Remove bread from pan; cool completely on wire rack.

Makes 1 loaf

Black Forest Banana Bread

CHOCOLATE CHIP SCONE MIX

2 cups all-purpose flour
1 cup mini semisweet chocolate chips
¾ cup golden raisins
½ cup sugar
2 teaspoons baking powder
¼ teaspoon salt
¼ teaspoon baking soda
¼ teaspoon ground cinnamon

1. Layer ingredients attractively in any order into 1-quart food storage jar with tight-fitting lid. Pack ingredients down slightly before adding another layer.

2. Cover top of jar with fabric; attach gift tag with raffia or ribbon.

Makes one 1-quart jar

CHOCOLATE CHIP SCONES

1 jar Chocolate Chip Scone Mix
½ cup (1 stick) butter, cut into small pieces
½ cup buttermilk
2 eggs, divided
½ teaspoon vanilla
1 tablespoon milk

1. Preheat oven to 350°F. Lightly grease two cookie sheets.

2. Pour contents of jar into large bowl. Cut in butter with pastry blender or 2 knives until mixture resembles coarse crumbs. Beat buttermilk, 1 egg and vanilla in small bowl. Add to flour mixture; mix just until sticky dough is formed. Using 2 tablespoons dough for each scone, drop dough onto prepared cookie sheets. Blend remaining egg and milk in small bowl; brush mixture over top of scones.

3. Bake 12 to 14 minutes or until toothpick inserted into centers comes out. Cool 5 minutes on wire rack. Serve warm.

Makes 2 dozen scones

Chocolate Chip Scones

EGGNOG CHERRY QUICK BREAD MIX

1 cup all-purpose flour
¾ cup sugar
½ cup chopped candied or dried cherries
¾ cup chopped pecans
1¼ cups all-purpose flour
1 tablespoon baking powder
1 teaspoon ground nutmeg
½ teaspoon salt

1. Layer all ingredients in the order listed above in 1-quart food storage jar with tight-fitting lid. Pack ingredients down lightly before adding another layer.

2. Cover top of jar with fabric; attach gift tag with raffia or ribbon.

Makes one 1-quart jar

Gift Idea: Assemble a gift basket with a jar of Eggnog Cherry Quick Bread Mix, a package of gourmet coffee or tea and 3 miniature (5½×3-inch) loaf pans.

EGGNOG CHERRY QUICK BREAD

1 jar Eggnog Cherry Quick Bread Mix
1¼ cups prepared dairy eggnog or half-and-half
2 eggs
6 tablespoons (¾ stick) butter, melted and cooled
1 teaspoon vanilla

1. Preheat oven to 350°F. Spray 3 miniature (5½×3-inch) loaf pans with nonstick cooking spray.

2. Place contents of jar into large bowl; stir until blended. Whisk together eggnog, eggs, butter and vanilla in separate bowl. Add eggnog mixture to flour mixture; stir just until moistened. Divide equally into prepared pans.

3. Bake 35 to 40 minutes or until toothpick inserted into centers comes out clean. Cool in pans 15 minutes. Remove from pans to wire racks; cool completely. Tightly wrap in plastic wrap; store at room temperature.

Makes 3 miniature loaves

Eggnog Cherry Quick Bread

CHOCOLATE CHUNK COFFEECAKE MIX

1¾ cups all-purpose flour
1 cup chocolate chunks
¾ cup packed brown sugar
½ cup chopped nuts
1 teaspoon baking powder
1 teaspoon baking soda
¼ teaspoon salt

1. Layer ingredients attractively in any order into 1-quart food storage jar with tight-fitting lid. Pack ingredients down tightly before adding another layer.

2. Cover top of jar with fabric; attach gift tag with raffia or ribbon.

Makes one 1-quart jar

CHOCOLATE CHUNK COFFEECAKE

½ cup (1 stick) butter, softened
3 eggs
1 teaspoon vanilla
1 jar Chocolate Chunk Coffeecake Mix
1 cup sour cream

1. Preheat oven to 350°F. Grease 13×9-inch baking pan.

2. Beat butter in large bowl until smooth. Beat in eggs and vanilla until blended. (Mixture may appear curdled.) Add coffeecake mix and sour cream; stir until well blended.

3. Spread batter evenly in prepared pan. Bake 25 to 35 minutes or until toothpick inserted into center comes out clean. Cool in pan on wire rack.

Makes 12 to 16 servings

Chocolate Chunk Coffeecake

LEMON RAISIN QUICK BREAD MIX

2 cups all-purpose flour
1 cup raisins
¾ cup chopped walnuts
⅓ cup packed brown sugar
2 teaspoons baking powder
½ teaspoon baking soda
¼ teaspoon salt

1. Layer ingredients attractively in any order in 1-quart food storage jar with tight-fitting lid. Pack ingredients down lightly before adding another layer.

2. Cover top of jar with fabric; attach gift tag with raffia or ribbon.

Makes one 1-quart jar

LEMON RAISIN QUICK BREAD

1 jar Lemon Raisin Quick Bread Mix
1½ cups lemon-flavored yogurt (not sugar-free)
¼ cup (½ stick) butter, melted and cooled slightly
1 egg

1. Preheat oven to 350°F. Spray 8½×4½-inch loaf pan with nonstick cooking spray.

2. Pour contents of jar into large bowl. Combine yogurt, butter and egg in small bowl until blended; stir into jar mixture just until moistened. Pour evenly into prepared pan and smooth top.

3. Bake 45 to 50 minutes or until toothpick inserted into center comes out clean. Cool in pan on wire rack 30 minutes. Remove from pan; cool completely on wire rack.

Makes 1 loaf

Lemon Raisin Quick Bread

CAKES & CUPCAKES

BANANA SNACK CAKE MIX

½ cup granulated sugar
¾ cup packed brown sugar
1¼ cups all-purpose flour
1 teaspoon baking powder
¾ teaspoon salt
½ teaspoon baking soda
½ cup chopped walnuts
1 cup semisweet chocolate chips

1. Layer ingredients attractively in any order in 1-quart food storage jar with tight-fitting lid. Pack ingredients down lightly before adding another layer.

2. Cover top of jar with fabric; attach gift tag with raffia and ribbon.

Makes one 1-quart jar

BANANA SNACK CAKE

1 jar Banana Snack Cake Mix
1¼ cups mashed ripe bananas (about 4 medium)
½ cup vegetable oil
2 eggs, beaten
1 teaspoon vanilla

1. Preheat oven to 350°F. Grease and flour 8- or 9-inch square baking pan.

2. Place contents of jar in large bowl. Add bananas, oil, eggs and vanilla; stir until well blended. Pour into prepared pan.

3. Bake 40 to 45 minutes or until toothpick inserted into center comes out clean. Cool completely in pan on wire rack.
Makes 9 to 12 servings

Banana Snack Cake

1 jar Banana Snack Cake Mix
1¼ cups mashed ripe bananas
(about 4 medium)
½ cup vegetable oil

2 eggs, beaten
1 teaspoon vanilla
Chocolate frosti

1. Preheat oven to 350°F. Grease and flour 9×9-inch baking
until well blended. Place contents of jar in large bowl. Add bananas, oil
3. Bake 40 to 45 minutes until 2. reated pan.
Cool completely in p

Mal 9 to 12 servings

BLACK BOTTOM CUPCAKE MIX

2 cups all-purpose flour
1 cup packed brown sugar
¾ cup unsweetened cocoa powder
½ cup granulated sugar
1 teaspoon baking powder
½ teaspoon baking soda
½ teaspoon salt

1. Layer ingredients attractively in any order into 1-quart food storage jar with tight-fitting lid. Pack ingredients down slightly before adding another layer.

2. Cover top of jar with fabric; attach gift tag with raffia or ribbon.

Makes one 1-quart jar

BLACK BOTTOM CUPCAKES

1 package (8 ounces) cream cheese, softened
4 eggs, divided
⅓ cup sugar
1 cup buttermilk
½ cup vegetable oil
1½ teaspoons vanilla
1 jar Black Bottom Cupcake Mix

1. Preheat oven to 350°F. Paper-line 20 standard (2½-inch) muffin cups.

2. Beat cream cheese, 1 egg and sugar in small bowl until smooth and creamy; set aside.

3. Beat buttermilk, remaining 3 eggs, oil and vanilla in large bowl until blended. Add contents of jar; beat 1 to 2 minutes or until well blended. Spoon batter into muffin cups, filling about ¾ full. Spoon heaping tablespoon cream cheese mixture over batter in each cup; gently swirl with tip of knife to marbleize.

4. Bake 20 to 25 minutes or until toothpick inserted into centers comes out clean. Cool in pans on wire racks 5 minutes. Remove from pans; cool completely on wire racks.

Makes 20 cupcakes

Black Bottom Cupcakes

MISTLETOE KISS ME CAKE MIX

1 cup sugar
1 cup all-purpose flour
1 teaspoon baking soda
1 teaspoon salt
1 teaspoon dried orange peel
½ teaspoon ground nutmeg
⅓ cup chopped walnuts
1 cup raisins, coarsely chopped
1 cup all-purpose flour
¼ cup sugar
1 teaspoon ground cinnamon

1. Layer all ingredients except ¼ cup sugar and cinnamon in the order listed above in wide-mouth 1-quart food storage jar with tight-fitting lid. Lightly pack down ingredients before adding another layer. Place sugar and cinnamon in small plastic food storage bag. Close with twist tie; cut off top of bag. Place bag in jar.

2. Cover top of jar with fabric; attach gift tag with raffia or ribbon.

Makes one 1-quart jar

MISTLETOE KISS ME CAKES

1 jar Mistletoe Kiss Me Cake Mix
½ cup (1 stick) butter, softened
2 eggs
½ cup milk
¾ cup orange juice, divided
2 teaspoons grated orange peel

1. Preheat oven to 350°F. Lightly grease and flour 6 (1-cup) mini bundt pan cups.

2. Remove cinnamon sugar packet from jar. Pour remaining contents of jar into medium bowl; stir until well blended. Beat butter in large bowl with electric mixer on medium speed until smooth. Beat in eggs, one at a time. Add milk, ½ cup orange juice and orange peel; beat until well blended. Gradually add flour mixture, beating until blended. Divide equally into prepared pans.

3. Bake 20 to 25 minutes or until toothpick inserted near centers comes out clean. Cool in pan 10 minutes. Loosen edges; remove cakes to wire rack. Cool completely.

4. Pour remaining ¼ cup juice over cakes. Sprinkle with cinnamon sugar.

Makes 6 mini bundt cakes

Mistletoe Kiss Me Cakes

PUMPKIN SNACK CAKE MIX

2 cups all-purpose flour
1 cup packed brown sugar
1 cup semisweet chocolate chips
½ cup chopped nuts
2 teaspoons baking powder
1½ teaspoons pumpkin pic spice
½ teaspoon baking soda
¼ teaspoon salt

1. Layer ingredients attractively in any order into 1-quart food storage jar with tight-fitting lid. Pack ingredients down tightly before adding another layer.

2. Cover top of jar with fabric; attach gift tag with raffia or ribbon.

Makes one 1-quart jar

PUMPKIN SNACK CAKE

1 cup (2 sticks) butter, softened
1 cup solid-pack pumpkin
2 eggs
1 teaspoon vanilla
1 jar Pumpkin Snack Cake Mix

1. Preheat oven to 350°F. Grease 9-inch square baking pan.

2. Beat butter in large bowl until smooth. Beat in pumpkin, eggs and vanilla until blended. Add cake mix to pumpkin mixture; stir until well blended. Spread batter into prepared pan.

3. Bake 40 to 45 minutes or until toothpick inserted into center comes out clean. Cool in pan on wire rack.

Makes 12 servings

Pumpkin Snack Cake

SWEETHEART CHOCOLATE MINI BUNDT CAKE MIX

1⅔ cups all-purpose flour
1 teaspoon baking soda
¼ teaspoon salt
¾ cup packed brown sugar
½ cup unsweetened cocoa powder
1 cup semisweet chocolate chips, divided

1. Combine flour, baking soda and salt in medium bowl. Layer ½ of flour mixture, brown sugar, remaining flour mixture, cocoa and ¾ cup chips in in 1-quart food storage jar with tight-fitting lid. Place remaining ½ cup chips in small plastic food storage bag. Seal bag; place in jar.

2. Cover top of jar with fabric. Attach gift tag to jar with raffia or ribbon.

Makes one 1-quart jar

SWEETHEART CHOCOLATE MINI BUNDT CAKES

¾ cup mayonnaise
1 cup plus 2 tablespoons buttermilk
1 teaspoon vanilla
1 jar Sweetheart Chocolate Mini Bundt Cake Mix
¼ cup whipping cream

1. Preheat oven to 350°F. Spray 6 mini bundt pan cups with nonstick cooking spray. Remove bag of chips from jar; set aside.

2. Beat mayonnaise in large bowl with electric mixer on low speed; beat in buttermilk and vanilla. Add remaining contents of jar to mayonnaise mixture; beat on low speed 30 seconds. Beat 1 minute on medium speed.

3. Spoon batter evenly into prepared pans. Bake 22 minutes until toothpick inserted near centers comes out clean. Cool in pans 15 minutes. Invert cakes onto wire rack.

4. Place remaining chips in small bowl. Heat cream in small saucepan over low heat until bubbles form around edge; pour over chips. Let stand 5 minutes; stir until smooth. Cool and drizzle over cakes.

Makes 6 mini bundt cakes

Sweetheart Chocolate Mini Bundt Cakes

VOLUME MEASUREMENTS (dry)

$^1/_8$ teaspoon = 0.5 mL
$^1/_4$ teaspoon = 1 mL
$^1/_2$ teaspoon = 2 mL
$^3/_4$ teaspoon = 4 mL
1 teaspoon = 5 mL
1 tablespoon = 15 mL
2 tablespoons = 30 mL
$^1/_4$ cup = 60 mL
$^1/_3$ cup = 75 mL
$^1/_2$ cup = 125 mL
$^2/_3$ cup = 150 mL
$^3/_4$ cup = 175 mL
1 cup = 250 mL
2 cups = 1 pint = 500 mL
3 cups = 750 mL
4 cups = 1 quart = 1 L

VOLUME MEASUREMENTS (fluid)

1 fluid ounce (2 tablespoons) = 30 mL
4 fluid ounces ($^1/_2$ cup) = 125 mL
8 fluid ounces (1 cup) = 250 mL
12 fluid ounces ($1^1/_2$ cups) = 375 mL
16 fluid ounces (2 cups) = 500 mL

WEIGHTS (mass)

$^1/_2$ ounce = 15 g
1 ounce = 30 g
3 ounces = 90 g
4 ounces = 120 g
8 ounces = 225 g
10 ounces = 285 g
12 ounces = 360 g
16 ounces = 1 pound = 450 g

DIMENSIONS

$^1/_{16}$ inch = 2 mm
$^1/_8$ inch = 3 mm
$^1/_4$ inch = 6 mm
$^1/_2$ inch = 1.5 cm
$^3/_4$ inch = 2 cm
1 inch = 2.5 cm

OVEN TEMPERATURES

250°F = 120°C
275°F = 140°C
300°F = 150°C
325°F = 160°C
350°F = 180°C
375°F = 190°C
400°F = 200°C
425°F = 220°C
450°F = 230°C

BAKING PAN SIZES

Utensil	Size in Inches/Quarts	Metric Volume	Size in Centimeters
Baking or Cake Pan (square or rectangular)	8×8×2	2 L	20×20×5
	9×9×2	2.5 L	23×23×5
	12×8×2	3 L	30×20×5
	13×9×2	3.5 L	33×23×5
Loaf Pan	8×4×3	1.5 L	20×10×7
	9×5×3	2 L	23×13×7
Round Layer Cake Pan	8×1½	1.2 L	20×4
	9×1½	1.5 L	23×4
Pie Plate	8×1¼	750 mL	20×3
	9×1¼	1 L	23×3
Baking Dish or Casserole	1 quart	1 L	—
	1½ quart	1.5 L	—
	2 quart	2 L	—